FORGIVENESS

RELEASING THE POWER OF GRACE

FRANK DAMAZIO

CityChristianPublishing

Published by
City Christian Publishing
9200 NE Fremont
Portland, Oregon 97220

City Christian Publishing is a ministry of City Bible Church and is dedicated to serving the local church and its leaders through the production and distribution of quality equipping resources. It is our prayer that these materials, proven in the context of the local church, will equip leaders in exalting the Lord and extending His kingdom.

For a free catalog of additional resources from City Christian Publishing, please call 1-800-777-6057 or visit our web site at www.CityChristianPublishing.com.

Forgiveness: Releasing the Power of Grace

Cover, Interior designed and typeset by City Christian Publishing.

First Edition, July 2007

Printed in the United States of America

Contents

Chapter 1

The Gift of Forgiveness

If the title of this book caught your attention, you could be one of two types of people. You could be the person who has been greatly hurt by someone very close to you, someone you trusted who stabbed you in the back. You picked this book up thinking, "Just try to convince me that I should forgive them." The person who hurt you is not repentant and doesn't care about the harm he or she has done to your life. Forgive? "When they come groveling at my feet, begging for my mercy, offering to compensate me for all the pain they've caused, then I'll think about it."

Or you could be the person who has been greatly hurt but doesn't know how to handle it. You know that you need to forgive and you want to, but you can't find it in you. The pain is too great. Every time you see that person the physical "flight" response in your body goes into overdrive and it's all you can do to not bolt and run from the room. Your mind says to forgive and you have tried to forgive, but your heart is too wounded to handle the thought.

You may be thinking that you haven't been hurt that deeply and you don't carry great offenses, so you don't have a problem with forgiveness. But you carry a chip on your shoulder, a "don't push me" attitude that withholds forgiveness from people so as to maintain control over your life – and over them. You expect people to treat you a certain way and if they don't, you hold it against them. You don't forgive.

For any type of person, the first thing you need to know is that forgiveness is necessary and it is possible. You don't enter the journey of forgiveness alone, but you walk through it with One who was beaten and tortured on behalf of others only to have them mock His sacrifice for them. In spite of that He chose to die for them – for you – forgiving them with His last breaths. Jesus is the One who forgives you and who gives you the grace necessary to forgive others.

What is forgiveness?

Forgiveness is a familiar word but it can mean something different to every person. To one person, forgiveness brings up wonderful memories of a time of reconciliation with a friend and the growth of a deep friendship from that experience. To another person, forgiveness brings up painful memories that cause the stomach to churn, the pulse to quicken and anxiety to rise.

Forgiveness affects everyone. It doesn't matter if your family background was wonderful or terrible, you still had to struggle with forgiveness. It doesn't matter your ethnic origin or your gender or your age, you have had to choose to forgive or not to forgive. Forgiveness touches every life – young and old, rich and poor, male and female. Some have to face it on a daily basis, others less frequently. Some have to face it on deep destructive issues, others on surface ones.

Whatever your place in life now, you must deal with the concept of forgiveness. How you deal with this word can either destroy your life or restore it. It can impact you spiritually, mentally, emotionally and physically. How you forgive can make you or break you. Forgiveness isn't a subject that we like to talk about, yet it is one of the key issues of kingdom living. No one is immune either to the need to forgive or to the devastating impact of not forgiving.

We talk about forgiveness casually in time-honored platitudes: Forgive and forget. Let bygones be bygones. Turn the other cheek. Kiss and make up. To err is human and to forgive is divine. But what is the truth about forgiveness? What does the Bible say?

Forgiveness is mentioned 124 times in the Bible. The first time is in Genesis 50:17 when Joseph's brothers beg him, "Please, forgive the trespass of the servants of the God of your father." The brothers had mocked Joseph, ridiculed him, and sold him into slavery. Now they came begging for mercy. Joseph's response was one of true forgiveness. "Am I God, to judge and punish you? As far as I am concerned, God turned into good what you meant for evil" (Genesis 50:19-20 New Living Translation).

The last time forgiveness is mentioned is in 1 John 1:9 when God promises, "If we confess our sins, he is faithful and just and will forgive us our sins and purify us from all unrighteousness."

These verses represent two sides of forgiveness – giving and receiving, and two types of forgiveness – human and divine.

The forgiven woman

In Luke 7 Jesus was having dinner at Simon the Pharisees' house when a "woman who was a sinner" began to wash his feet with her tears, wipe them with her hair and then anoint them with oil. Jesus used this as an opportunity to make a point with this story:

> " 'There was a certain creditor who had two debtors. One owed five hundred denarii, and the other fifty. And when they had nothing with which to repay, he freely forgave them both. Tell Me, therefore, which of them will love him more?' Simon answered and said, 'I suppose the one whom he forgave more.' And He said to him, 'You have rightly judged.'
>
> "Then He turned to the woman and said to Simon, 'Do you see this woman? I entered your house; you gave Me no water for My feet, but she has washed My feet with her tears and wiped them with the hair of her head. You gave Me no kiss, but this woman has not ceased to kiss My feet since the time I came in. You did not anoint My head with oil, but this woman has anointed My feet with fragrant oil. Therefore I say to you, her sins, which are many, are forgiven, for she loved much. But to whom little is forgiven, the same loves little' "(Luke 7:41-47).

She was forgiven much so she loved much. Do you love much because you have realized the deep forgiveness of God? Is there a reality in you that has received so much of the remission of sin and the cleansing of God that you have a gratefulness in you that pours out in extravagant love? The depth of forgiveness you have received has a direct relationship to your ability to love. If you have a difficult time loving, you have a difficult time understanding the greatness of God's forgiveness for you. When you receive divine forgiveness, you can give forgiveness to those around you.

The forgiven becomes the forgiver

Those who accept forgiveness adopt an attitude toward themselves that transforms their attitude toward others. They have such a deep well of gratitude that it is easy for them to reach inside and draw out forgiveness to dispense to others. Receiving forgiveness changes you. The woman in Luke 7 knew how great her sin was. She also knew how great was the love that forgave her sin. She had experienced forgiveness to a depth that changed her life. Psychiatrist Karl Menninger once said that if he could convince his psychiatric hospital patients that their sins were forgiven, three quarters of them could walk out the next day.

Illumination of darkness

We have total forgiveness through salvation. It is through salvation that we receive the forgiveness of all our sins, all our wrongdoings, all our past. The first thing that happens at salvation is illumination. Our inner darkness and spiritual blindness can be overcome by the illumination of the Holy Spirit. You cannot receive God's forgiveness until you know you have sinned, but our minds are blinded to the truth and we live unforgiven in our sin.

2 Corinthians 4:4 says, "whose minds the god of this age has blinded, who do not believe, lest the light of the gospel of the glory of Christ, who is the image of God, should shine on them." We are blinded to the truth, blinded to Christ. But Paul goes on to say in verse 6, "For it is the God who commanded light to shine out of darkness, who has shone in our hearts to give the light of the knowledge of the glory of God in the face of Jesus Christ."

Every person needs a sharp awareness that before a holy and loving God they are a sinner in desperate plight and needing salvation.

Conviction of sin

Conviction is an action of the Spirit, not of our mind. It is the action of the Spirit that brings about a profound inner sense of quiet before God and a deep conviction of one's sinfulness. It is not just feeling miserable or remorseful. It is not sorrow for being caught or pain because of the consequences. Conviction comes through the illumination of the Holy Spirit into our spirit so that we realize before a loving and holy God there is no way we can change ourselves. Conviction comes with a realization that I am a sinner and I cannot change that on my own. It is a sorrow and grief that turns a person toward God as in Acts 2:37: "Now when they heard this, they were cut to the heart, and said to Peter and the rest of the apostles, 'Men and brethren, what shall we do?'"

Repentance from sin

Conviction of sin leads us to repentance. Repentance is an act of the will to turn from sin. It is turning from the old way of life to a new way of life in God. In Acts 2:37 the people were "cut to the heart." Their conviction went straight into the core of who they were, but it lead to repentance.

The first words out of their mouth were, "What shall we do?" They knew they had sinned. They knew they were wrong and they wanted to turn to God and to do what was right. Conviction isn't enough. They could have felt the sorrow for their guilt, but unless they had acted there would have been no change.

Repentance is an act of the will strengthened by the Holy Spirit that moves the whole life away from sin toward God. Peter responded to their question with a simple declaration, "Repent, and let every one of you be baptized in the name of Jesus Christ for the remission of sins; and you shall receive the gift of the Holy Spirit" (Acts 2:38).

Faith in God

Salvation does not happen when you say, "I'm really sorry for my sin and I hope I don't go to hell." Salvation is not just saying the words but continuing old actions. Faith is looking to God and acting on that belief. Acts 20:21 says "testifying to Jews, and also to

Greeks, repentance toward God and faith toward our Lord Jesus Christ."

Conversion

Conversion is a total alteration that includes all the above, resulting in a changed life. Conversion is when your actions give reality to your repentance. Acts 3:19 says, "Repent therefore and be converted, that your sins may be blotted out, so that times of refreshing may come from the presence of the Lord."

Whatever is in your life that is not in agreement with the word of God, you lay it aside. You change your old lifestyle. Romans 10:9-10 says, "If you confess with your mouth the Lord Jesus and believe in your heart that God has raised Him from the dead, you will be saved. For with the heart one believes unto righteousness, and with the mouth confession is made unto salvation."

Justification

When you are justified, you have right-standing before God. You have been acquitted. You have been pronounced righteous and declared to be righteous by God. You may not feel righteous, but justification has nothing to do with your feelings. It has nothing to do with how much you sinned or how big your sins were. A six-year-old child who has just accepted Christ is justified the same as a 45-year-old convict who has accepted Christ. Small sin or big sin, 50 days of sin or 50 years of sin, when you are acquitted, all of the sin is gone. You stand holy and justified before God, acknowledged as righteous because of His righteousness given to you. You are accepted and forgiven.

The ground of our justification is God's act of redemption in Jesus Christ. We have all fallen short of the glory of God. We are justified by His grace as a gift. Romans 4:5 says, "But to him who does not work but believes on Him who justifies the ungodly, his faith is accounted for righteousness."

A new heart

God promises in Ezekiel 36:26: "I will give you a new heart and put a new spirit within you; I will take the heart of stone out of your flesh and give you a heart of flesh." Instead of the old person with its sinful desperation, attitudes, and impulses, there emerges a new self with new power in the Holy Spirit. You have the power to live a righteous life.

As a new creation, you have a new heart, a heart that has been forgiven. Like the woman in Luke 7, you have been forgiven much and you love much. You, the forgiven, can now become the forgiver.

Washed out with the tide

Chuck Colson gives a profound example of the forgiveness of God.

"The blood of Jesus is sufficient for the forgiveness of any and all sins because the Cross was two thousand years ago and all of our sins were still to come. Therefore, all of our sins, whether we committed them yesterday or today or have yet to commit them tomorrow, are covered by His blood—past sins, present sins, future sins, big sins, small sins, or medium-size sins—it makes no difference.

"A few years ago, I found myself groping for a way to explain this to a woman who had been on death row for multiple murders and would be executed within ten hours of my visit. Tears glistened in her eyes as she looked at me beseechingly, needing assurance of the salvation she had claimed by faith six years earlier. That very night she would be stepping into eternity, and she was desperate for reassurance of her forgiveness by God.

"I asked her if she had ever been to the ocean, and she nodded yes. I asked her if, as she had walked along the shore, she had seen small holes in the sand where ghost crabs had darted in and out. Again she nodded affirmatively. I then asked if she had seen any larger holes, like those made by children digging a deep moat around a sandcastle. Beginning to look somewhat puzzled, she said yes, she had seen holes like that. I persisted as I probed gently to see if she had ever seen huge holes created by machines dredging a channel or burying pipe lines on the beach. Her brow began to furrow as she again acknowledged a quiet yes. I then leaned toward her and pressed my point, 'Velma, when the tide comes in, what happens to all those holes? The little ones made by the crabs, and the medium-size ones made by children, and the great big ones made by machines?'

"A soft light began to gleam in her eyes, and a smile played at the corner of her lips as I answered my own question: 'All the holes are covered equally by the water, aren't they? The blood of Jesus is like the tide that washes over the "holes" of your sins and covers all your sins equally.' And Velma stepped into eternity reassured of her forgiveness by God and a welcome into her heavenly home based on nothing but the blood of Jesus!"[1]

Forgiveness in God

Ephesians 1:7-8 says, "In Him we have redemption through His blood, the forgiveness of sins, according to the riches of His grace which He made to abound toward us in all wisdom and prudence." According to the riches of His grace, you are forgiven. It isn't just a little bit of forgiveness. He doesn't pour a little bit of the ocean into the cavernous hole that your sins have dug, but He pours in a flood-tide of forgiveness that completely covers your sin.

Before turning to the next chapter, carefully read and reflect on the following scriptures. Whether you are a seasoned veteran of Christianity or a brand-new believer, the power of the forgiveness of God in your life is enduring. God forgives you always. He didn't just forgive you when you got saved. He still forgives you now.

Psalm 103:3,10-14

"Who forgives all your iniquities, who heals all your diseases... He has not dealt with us according to our sins, nor punished us according to our iniquities. For as the heavens are high above the earth, so great is His mercy toward those who fear Him; as far as the east is from the west, so far has He removed our transgressions from us.

As a father pities his children, so the Lord pities those who fear Him. For He knows our frame; He remembers that we are dust."

Psalm 130:3-4

"If You, Lord, should mark iniquities, O Lord, who could stand? But there is forgiveness with You, that You may be feared."

Isaiah 43:25

"I, even I, am He who blots out your transgressions for My own sake; and I will not remember your sins."

Isaiah 1:18

" 'Come now, and let us reason together,' says the Lord, 'Though your sins are like scarlet, they shall be as white as snow; though they are red like crimson, they shall be as wool.' "

Isaiah 44:22

"I have blotted out, like a thick cloud, your transgressions, and like a cloud, your sins. Return to Me, for I have redeemed you."

Jeremiah 50:20

*"'In those days and in that time,' says the Lord,
'The iniquity of Israel shall be sought, but there
shall be none; and the sins of Judah, but they
shall not be found; for I will pardon those whom
I preserve.'"*

Jeremiah 31:34

*"'No more shall every man teach his neighbor,
and every man his brother, saying, "Know the
Lord," for they all shall know Me, from the least of
them to the greatest of them,' says the Lord. 'For
I will forgive their iniquity, and their sin I will remember no more.'"*

Micah 7:18-19

*"Who is a God like You, pardoning iniquity and
passing over the transgression of the remnant of
His heritage? He does not retain His anger forever, because He delights in mercy. He will again
have compassion on us, and will subdue our iniquities. You will cast all our sins into the depths
of the sea."*

Matthew 26:28

"For this is My blood of the new covenant, which is shed for many for the remission of sins."

Romans 4:7

"Blessed are those whose lawless deeds are forgiven, and whose sins are covered."

Colossians 1:14

"...in whom we have redemption through His blood, the forgiveness of sins."

Acts 10:43

"To Him all the prophets witness that, through His name, whoever believes in Him will receive remission of sins."

Acts 26:18

"To open their eyes, in order to turn them from darkness to light, and from the power of Satan to God, that they may receive forgiveness of sins

and an inheritance among those who are sanctified by faith in Me."

Hebrews 10:16-17

" 'This is the covenant that I will make with them after those days,' says the Lord: 'I will put My laws into their hearts, and in their minds I will write them,' then He adds, 'Their sins and their lawless deeds I will remember no more.' "

Chapter 2

Receiving God's Forgiveness

Forgiveness is all about freedom. When you are forgiven, you are freed from the prison of sin and bondage. You have been released to step out into a new life in God. But forgiveness does not stop with you. The forgiven person must in turn be a forgiver.

Some people accept God's forgiveness. They become the forgiven, but they will not become a forgiver. They have tasted of the powerful forgiveness of God but they will not release that same power to those around them – their spouse, their mother, their father, their siblings, their boss, their friend. What does God command? "Be kind to one another, tenderhearted, *forgiving* one another, even as God in Christ forgave you" (Ephesians 4:32). We are commanded to forgive as we have been forgiven.

Top 20 difficult life situations

Someone once wrote a list of the top twenty most difficult things to do in life. The first one is to apologize. The list continues: To begin over, to be unselfish, to take advice, to admit error, to face a sneer, to think and then act, to be charitable, to keep trying, to be considerate, to avoid mistakes, to endure success, to profit by mistakes, to keep out of a rut, to make the best of just a little, to subdue an unruly temper, to shoulder deserved blame, to recognize a silver lining.

Those are the first eighteen, but the final two strike home: to receive forgiveness and to give forgiveness.

What is forgiveness?

Forgiveness is pardoning an offender so that he is considered and treated not guilty. It is to stop blaming others for something they have done. To forgive is to give up the power and desire to punish.

The various Hebrew words for forgiveness stress the idea of wiping out or blotting out the memory of the sin, covering or concealing it. It can mean bestowing pardon on the basis of a substitute who takes the punishment.

The Greek carries the connotation of forgiveness as setting free or liberating someone from prison, canceling their debt and letting them go as if they had not committed a crime. It carries the concept of grace.

Cleansed by the blood of Jesus

Sin is a transgression, a breaking of the law. It is the act. Iniquity is the evil born within us that breeds the sin. Iniquities are the sinful habits and traits that are inbred into our very nature.

Romans 5:12 states, "Therefore, just as through one man sin entered the world, and death through sin, and thus death spread to all men, because all sinned..." Adam sinned in the garden of Eden and passed iniquity to all mankind. Psalm 51:5 says, "I was brought forth in iniquity..." The Bible sometimes refers to this as "the old man" or "the body of sin."

But Isaiah tells us that Jesus took our iniquities on the cross. He had never sinned, but He paid the price for our iniquities. There is a picture of this in the Old Testament. In Leviticus 16:21, Aaron, the high priest, makes a sacrifice for the sins of the nation of Israel. He lays "both his hands on the head of the live goat, confesses over it all the iniquities of the children of Israel, and all their transgressions, concerning all their sins, putting them on the head of the goat, and shall send it into the wilderness..."

This had to be done every year. It wasn't a permanent solution, but one that pointed forward to the day that Jesus would be the Lamb of God who takes away the sin of the world (John 1:29). Isaiah 53:11 declares, "My righteous Servant shall justify many, for He shall bear their iniquities."

Micah 7:18-19 says God pardons us with delight: "Who is a God like You, pardoning iniquity and passing over the transgression of the remnant of His heritage? He does not retain His anger forever, because He delights in mercy. He will again have compassion on us, and will subdue our iniquities. You will cast all our sins into the depths of the sea."

The blood of Jesus forgives all your sin and cancels your debt. But we must accept it. 1 John 1:9 says, "If we confess our sins, He is faithful and just to forgive us our sins and to cleanse us from all unrighteousness." If we confess, He will forgive. In Proverbs 28:13 God promises, "He who covers his sins will not prosper, but whoever confesses and forsakes them will have mercy."

Colossians 2:13-14 tells us, "You, being dead in your trespasses and the uncircumcision of your flesh, He has made alive together with Him, having forgiven you all trespasses, having wiped out the handwriting of requirements that was against us, which was contrary to us. And He has taken it out of the way, having nailed it to the cross."

Forgiveness cancels our debt. In New Testament times, if a man owed someone, he would write out a debt certificate of all that was owed. When the debt was paid in full, he would nail that certificate up in a public place for everyone to know that he was free from that debt certificate. When you place your trust in the blood of Jesus that paid your debt, you can nail up your debt certificate on the cross.

God's forgiveness is complete

Unlike man's forgiveness, God's forgiveness completely removes your sin. When He forgives, the debt is completely wiped clean.

Martin Luther once dreamed that the devil was unrolling a large scroll and reading his sins off one-by-one. He reached the end of the scroll and Martin Luther asked, "Is that all?" "Oh no," the devil replied and began reading a second scroll. He finished reading that one and again Luther questioned, "Is that all?" The devil laughed and began reading a third scroll. But finally, he finished the third scroll and had no more. In his dream Luther exclaimed triumphantly, "Quick! Write on each of them, 'The blood of Jesus Christ God's son cleanses us from all sin!'"

There are no scrolls left for the devil to read against you. There is nothing he can dig up and hold over your head. Your sins are forgiven in God. God forgives completely, wiping out the sin. Hebrews 10:16-17 reads, " 'This is the covenant that I will make with them after those days,' says the Lord: 'I will put My laws into their hearts, and in their minds I will write them,' then He adds, *Their sins and their lawless deeds I will remember no more.'* "

The power of forgetting

There was a priest who was a much-loved man of God, looked up to and admired by everyone, but deep in his heart he carried a heavy burden. Many years earlier, he had committed a secret sin. Even though he had confessed it to God, he still carried the weight in his spirit.

In his parish there was a woman who claimed to have visions in which Christ spoke with her and she with him. The priest was skeptical and decided to test her to see if she was making this up or if it was true, so he told her, "Next time you have a vision and speak with Christ, ask him what sin I committed while I was in seminary." She agreed.

Several days later she came to the priest and told him that Christ had appeared once more to her in her dreams. "Did you ask him what sin I committed?" "Yes," she replied. "Well, what did He say?" the priest asked. The woman responded, "He said, 'I don't remember.'"

As the Lord covenanted in Hebrews, "Their sins and their lawless deeds I will remember no more."

God forgives you eagerly

This is the greatness of God's forgiveness for you. This is exactly what He has done for you. Ephesians 4:32 says, "...forgiving one another, even as God in Christ forgave you." Psalm 86:5 tells us, "For You, Lord, are good, and ready to forgive, and abundant in mercy to all those who call upon You."

We have a God who is abundant in mercy, who is overflowing in grace. He is ready to forgive. He isn't reluctant or unwilling. He doesn't forgive out of obligation and duty. He is ready and willing, eager to forgive.

Forgiveness must be accepted

In 1830 George Wilson was convicted and sentenced to be hanged for his crimes. His influential friends began lobbying for a presidential pardon and soon obtained one from President Andrew Jackson. Wilson was going to die but he had been pardoned. His partner in crime had already been hung, a fate that he could now escape. But Wilson refused to accept it.

The question was sent to the Supreme Court. Can a person be forced to accept a pardon? Their decision was "a pardon is a deed, to the validity of which delivery is essential, and delivery is not complete without acceptance. It may then be rejected by the person to whom it is tendered; and if it is rejected, we have discovered no power in this court to force it upon him."[2]

Like George Wilson, you have the right to choose to accept pardon or reject it. You can accept Christ's forgiveness and His sacrifice for you or reject it. The Psalmist cried out, "Have mercy upon me, O God, according to Your lovingkindness; according to the multitude of Your tender mercies, blot out my transgressions" (Psalm 51:1). God has a multitude of mercy, an abundance of loving kindness, extended toward you. Accept it.

Oswald Chambers said it is not our regret about sinning but our acceptance that Jesus died for our sins that gives us forgiveness: "We trample the blood of the Son of God if we think we are forgiven because we are sorry for our sins. The only explanation for the forgiveness of God and for the unfathomable depth of His forgetting is the death of Jesus Christ. Our repentance is merely the outcome of our personal realization of the atonement which He has worked out for us. It does not matter who or what we are; there is absolute reinstatement into God by the death of Jesus Christ and by no other way, not because Jesus Christ pleads, but because He died. It is not earned, but accepted."[3]

Cultivating a forgiving spirit

Cultivating a forgiving spirit begins with embracing a forgiving Father.

Perhaps your earthly father was not a forgiving man and you have a hard time trusting your heavenly Father because of that. Perhaps your father was one who never spoke words of love, never gave you his time. Maybe he walked out of your home and your life and you never knew him. Maybe he was a harsh disciplinarian that you lived in fear of, but never learned to love.

Embrace the reality that God is different than every earthly father. He will never let you down and never turn a deaf ear to you. He will never give up on you. He will never abuse you. He is a loving Father who extends forgiveness, grace and mercy. You are forgiven by a Father who loves you with unlimited love. He never gets tired of forgiving you. His patience is inexhaustible.

A mother with exhausted patience had taken her son grocery shopping with her and was not having a good day. He was putting his hands into everything until his exasperated mother sternly commanded him not to touch anything else. She turned around to take a box of cereal off the shelf only to hear a tremendous crash. Spinning around she saw her son standing in front of a display with one can of chili in his hand while a hundred others lay scattered at his feet.

Beet red with embarrassment and anger, she stormed down the aisle, picked him up and put him in the seat of the grocery cart. "Don't you dare move a muscle! Don't talk. Don't wiggle. Don't move!" Silently the little boy watched as she began picking up the cans. After a few minutes, he asked her softly, "Mommy, you said the other day that when God forgives our sins He buries them at the bottom of the deepest ocean didn't you?"

"Yes," she hissed.

"And you said that it didn't matter what we did, God would never drag those things up again didn't you?" he continued.

Still frustrated, but unsure where he was going with this, she replied, "Yes."

"Well," he said, "I've got a feeling when we get home you're going to go fishing."

Aren't you glad God doesn't go fishing?

An unshakable love

You are loved by a Father who knows you. He knows your weaknesses and He still loves you. He rejoices when you turn from your sin and weeps over you when you do not.

Romans 8:35, 38-39 makes a bold and powerful statement. "Who shall separate us from the love of Christ? Shall tribulation, or distress, or persecution, or famine, or nakedness, or peril, or sword? ... For I am persuaded that neither death nor life, nor angels nor principalities nor powers, nor things present nor things to come, nor height nor depth, nor any other created thing, shall be able to separate us from the love of God which is in Christ Jesus our Lord."

Jesus tried to illustrate how much God loves us in Luke 15. This is the story of the father of the prodigal son. The boy had rebelled against the father, taken everything and left. He had ridiculed his father and humiliated him, mocked him with his lifestyle and made him the laughingstock of the town. Finally, he realized the foolishness and waste of his life and returned to his father.

The father owed the son nothing. He had already given him his inheritance. He didn't have to take him back. He could have disowned him. Instead Luke 15:20 says, "But when he (the son) was still a great way off, his father saw him and had compassion and ran and fell on his neck and kissed him." He didn't reluctantly forgive. He didn't accept him back with restrictions. He poured out an overflowing heart of fatherly love upon his son.

He didn't remind him of how he had blown it. Tell the son how much he had cost him. He didn't place conditions on the son's return. "You can come back but I don't trust you so I'm going to ..." No, he grabbed his son and held him and loved him. He gave him new clothes, a new identity. He gave him a new ring, entrusting him with his authority. He threw a party for everyone to see that he was publicly acknowledging his son again, making a public statement of his deep love and affection for him and his forgiveness for everything in the past.

This is how much God loves you.

Living like you are forgiven

Don't be like George Wilson who died with a presidential pardon in his hand. You have been given grace. You have been given forgiveness, but you must accept it. You don't have to do a certain number of good deeds each day to earn a place of forgiveness in God. You can't pay Christ back for the blood He shed for you. The pardon is in your hand. You simply have to accept it.

You may not feel as if you are forgiven. The prodigal son didn't feel forgiven. He came home groveling before his father, but his father lifted him to his feet and embraced him. God lifts you to your feet and embraces you. He places a ring on your finger and new clothes on your back. He makes the statement for everyone to see, "This is my child. I love him. I accept her. They are mine."

The prodigal son could have left the party and went out to sit in the pigpen again because he didn't feel as if he deserved the love and forgiveness of his father. And he didn't deserve it, but that's what makes it unconditional love. Instead the prodigal chose to accept his father's forgiveness. He chose to respond to his father's love and he lived once again as a beloved child of his father.

You can return to your pigpen or you can accept the love and forgiveness of your heavenly Father and begin to live as His child. He has given you the pardon. He has welcomed you home. It is your choice now. Will you come in to the party He has thrown for you or wallow in condemnation? You choose.

Chapter 3

Defining Forgiveness

The more I study forgiveness, the more difficult it is to wrap my mind around what it means. It seems too drastic. My sins are totally wiped out. There is no record of them anywhere.

That's hard to accept. We tend to think God's forgiveness is like ours. We forgive reluctantly and partially, holding it over the person's head until we feel they have been sufficiently punished. But Ephesians 1:7-8 tells of forgiveness given with grace and abundance. Abundant forgiveness from a rich supply of grace.

Once we are able to grasp and accept that overwhelming forgiveness, we can become forgivers. God gives us a new heart and the power to forgive is in us. It is not in our own power, but in the power of Christ in us. Ephesians 4:32 tells us to "be kind to one another, tenderhearted, forgiving one another, even as God in Christ forgave you."

Our standard of forgiveness should be "even as" God forgives us. Our forgiveness flows from a heart that grasps the overwhelming, unfathomable, incomprehensible forgiveness God gave us.

Forgiveness allows you to become a forgiver

Andrew Murray said, "He who only seeks forgiveness from selfishness and as freedom from punishment, but has not truly accepted forgiving love to rule his heart and life, proves that God's forgiveness has never really reached him. He who, on the other hand, has really accepted forgiveness will have in the joy with which he forgives others, a continual confirmation, that his faith in God's forgiveness of himself is a reality. From Christ to receive forgiveness, and like Christ to bestow it on others: these two are one."[4]

When we receive God's forgiveness, we are able to forgive. Not only are we able to forgive, but we are commanded to forgive others *just as* He forgave us.

Peter couldn't quite grasp this concept and in Matthew 18:21-22 Peter questioned Jesus, "Lord, how often shall my brother sin against me, and I forgive him? Up to seven times?" He was being very magnanimous. He was willing to forgive someone for the same offense seven times. Wasn't that great? Then Jesus blew Peter's magnanimity out of the water and said to him, "I do not say to you, up to seven times, but up to seventy times seven." That's a lot of forgiveness!

As we experience the awesome forgiveness of God, we can put our past into its proper perspective and realize that injuries and injustices are part of life. Resentment is a focus on the mistreatment that we have received from others. It is seeing the wrongs that have been done and harboring the pain of those experiences.

But forgiveness is lifting our eyes to the cross of Christ. Forgiveness is at the foot of the cross of One who was beaten, abused, mocked, humiliated in our place. Forgiveness is looking up into the eyes of One who never treated anyone unfairly yet is now suffering the greatest of agonies because of us and hearing Him say "You are forgiven."

If you have truly grasped the overwhelming reality of His love and forgiveness for you, can you then turn to one who has slighted you and demand punishment for them?

Remember the story of the woman in Luke 7 and Jesus' conclusion? "To whom little is forgiven, the same loves little." To whom much is forgiven, the same person loves much and forgives much.

Releasing resentment

When you become a forgiver, you do not hold on to grudges, hatred, self-pity or the need to punish other people. A bird called the Clark's Nutcracker collects up to 33,000 pine seeds and buries them in groups of three and four seeds in about 7,000 locations. It has such an amazing memory that during the course of the winter, it returns to every one of those 7,000 stockpiles to dig up and eat the seeds.

Some people do the same thing with hurts. They store them away, hoarding those offenses, hanging on to those resentments. Periodically they go dig those up and feed on them, nurturing the bitterness inside.

Galatians 5:14-15 warns us, "For all the law is fulfilled in one word, even in this: 'You shall love your neighbor as yourself.' But if you bite and devour one another, beware lest you be consumed by one another!' "

They say that if a rattlesnake is cornered, it will sometimes become so angry that it begins to bite itself. That is what resentment does. You cannot hurt the person who has wounded you, so you build up the resentment inside and begin to strike out in anger. The problem is that you are only harming yourself, not them. Someone once said that resentment is like taking poison and waiting for the other person to die. You strike out in anger, but harm only yourself.

Matthew 6:14-15 says, "For if you forgive men their trespasses, your heavenly Father will also forgive you. But if you do not forgive men their trespasses, neither will your Father forgive your trespasses."

Rediscover lost strength and energy

When you nurture unforgiveness and resentment, you waste your strength and energy. The Psalmist realized this when he said, "When I kept silent, my bones grew old through my groaning all the day long. For day and night Your hand was heavy upon me; my vitality was turned into the drought of summer. I acknowledged my sin to You, and my iniquity I have not hidden. I said, 'I will confess my transgressions to the Lord,' and You forgave the iniquity of my sin" (Psalm 32:3-5).

Dr. Lubetkin, a psychologist, says, "Holding a grudge takes mental, emotional and physical energy. It makes you obsessive, angry and depressed. There's a strong connection between anger and a wide spectrum of health miseries – chronic stomach upset, heart problems and skin conditions among them."[5]

Or as the old Chinese proverb says, "The man who opts for revenge should dig two graves."

Let go of your past and get on with your life

After the Civil War, Robert E. Lee had lunch at the home of a wealthy Kentucky widow. As they ate, she pointed to a magnolia tree that had been badly burned and charred by Northern artillery fire. In anger and sadness, she mourned the loss of this once-majestic tree that had been a part of their family memories for generations and condemned the cruelty of those who had destroyed this part of her life.

Pausing, she waited for General Lee to support her bitterness toward the North that had destroyed so many of their homes in the war. After pausing for several seconds, Lee said, "My dear madam, cut it down and forget it."

There are some things in life that we have to cut down and forget. Stop treasuring those reminders of past hurts and move on with life. Psalm 146:7 says, that God "executes justice for the oppressed, gives food to the hungry. The Lord gives freedom to the prisoners." Leave justice in God's hand and accept the freedom that forgiveness brings.

Physical and emotional healing

Forgiveness is good for your health, especially as preventive medicine. It aids the immune system. As I was reading through a medical journal I found unforgiveness paired with many problems: unforgiveness and lower back pain, unforgiveness and ulcers, unforgiveness and high blood pressure. You can go online and find institutions and organizations on forgiveness to teach you how to forgive. I went to Barnes and Nobles and asked for books on forgiveness. They gave me five pages of book titles.

Charlotte vanOyen Witvliet has demonstrated that unforgiving thoughts increase heart rate and blood pressure. In her work with Vietnam combat veterans, she learned that those who forgave themselves and others were less likely to suffer depression and post-traumatic stress disorder. [6]

Researchers at the University of Michigan's Institute for Social Research found that forgiveness was linked with better self-reported mental and physical health, especially for adults over 45. Respondents reporting higher levels of forgiveness were more satisfied with their lives and less likely to experience symptoms of psychological distress, such as nervousness, restlessness and sadness.[7]

A key to warmer, healthier relationships

Narvaez, a Spanish patriot, was dying. His father-confessor asked him if he had forgiven all his enemies. He replied, "I have no enemies, I have shot them all." This is *not* the key to building strong friendships!

Christ's key to relationships is seen in Colossians 3:12-14, "As the elect of God, holy and beloved, put on tender mercies, kindness, humility, meekness, longsuffering; bearing with one another, and forgiving one another, if anyone has a complaint against another; even as Christ forgave you, so you also must do. But above all these things put on love, which is the bond of perfection."

Marghanita Laski, a secular humanist, once said, "What I envy most about you Christians is your forgiveness. I have nobody to forgive me." The knowledge that someone loves you enough to forgive you builds trust and strengthens relationships and gives you the power to forgive others.

Forgiveness: Releasing the Power of Grace

Chapter 4

An Unforgiving Spirit

We can choose to be a forgiver or we can refuse to let go of the offense and the offender. The unforgiving person gives no pardon, no mercy, no forgiveness. He refuses to let go of past hurts and injustices.

Jesus warns us in Matthew 6:15 that "if you do not forgive men their trespasses, neither will your Father forgive your trespasses." No matter how you analyze, dissect and attempt to explain this verse, it comes down to one simple fact: if you don't forgive, the Father can't forgive you. This is a serious issue.

Ephesians 4:30-31 gives a similar warning: "And do not grieve the Holy Spirit of God, by whom you were sealed for the day of redemption. Let all bitterness, wrath, anger, clamor and evil speaking be put away from you, with all malice." Don't grieve the Holy Spirit. Don't block what He wants to do in your life. Don't cause Him sorrow because of your bitterness and unforgiveness.

But what if someone is a repeat offender? What if they constantly mistreat you? Do you have to keep forgiving them or is there a limit to how much you have to forgive? Peter felt he had a good limit when he asked in Matthew 18:21, "Lord, how often shall my brother sin against me, and I forgive him? Up to seven times?"

Forgiving someone for the same thing seven times seems like a very gracious thing to do and would require a lot of love and mercy. But that wasn't enough for Jesus. He said, "I do not say to you, up to seven times, but up to seventy times seven."

Seventy times seven. He wasn't telling Peter to count each time he forgave and then stop when he hit 490. He was saying forgive without limit because that is how God has forgiven you.

Forgiving as you are forgiven

Dave was facing a serious problem. He had gotten into trouble with the stock market and had borrowed money from his employer to get himself out of the hole. But he was in so deep there was no way out. By the time the employer was fed up with him, his debt was $15 million. He had about as much chance to pay that off as a hippopatumus has to fly

– none. He did the only thing he could do. He went to his employer and confessed what he had done and the extent to which he was in debt.

His boss was livid. He picked up the phone to call the police and have Dave prosecuted, but Dave begged him, "Please don't do this! Who will take care of my family if I go to jail? I'll pay you back. I'll sell everything I have and work two jobs. I'll pay you as much as I can every week for the rest of my life until this debt is paid. I promise!"

His boss knew he couldn't repay a fraction of the debt, but his heart went out to Dave and he told him, "Consider your debt forgiven. I won't report you to the police. I won't require payment and I won't fire you. I forgive it."

Dave couldn't believe his ears. Ecstatic, he ran out the door to go tell his wife the good news. Fifteen million dollar debt forgiven. They could start over. They could do it right this time, no gambling, no stealing. They had been given a fresh start! It was a new day – a good day!

As Dave entered the elevator, he caught sight of Phil who used to work in the cubicle next to his. His attitude immediately changed. Phil was always borrowing money from him and several months ago he had borrowed $15 for lunch and never paid Dave back. Dave had nagged him about it for weeks and Phil had promised to pay him. Then Phil had been transferred to another department and wouldn't return Dave's phone calls. Dave sent emails and left messages. He even went out of his way to go down to Phil's new office and put a note on the door, but Phil ignored him.

Dave was fed up. The months of resentment burst to the surface at the sight of his one-time friend and he pushed him against the wall of the elevator. "You will pay me that $15 and you will pay me now. I have a signed IOU from you and I will take you to court and have your check garnished if necessary, but you will pay me! I'm fed up with your mooching and avoiding me. You know you owe me so pay up now!"

Sound familiar? This is an updated version of the story Jesus tells in Matthew 18 of the unforgiving servant. His conclusion was, "Should you not also have had compassion on your fellow servant, just as I had pity on you?" (Matthew 18:33).

Just as Dave had been forgiven without limit, he was to forgive Phil. But how often do we accept Christ's unconditional forgiveness then refuse to forgive those who have hurt us? Our hurt is too great and our pain is too raw so we nurture our offense and will not forgive.

Holding on to past disappointments

Disappointments can be difficult to forgive. You can experience small disappointments that build up over time into a large obstacle or you can have a huge disappointment that overwhelms you.

One woman had bitterness toward her father going back over 25 years. Her parents had divorced and re-married when she was just a child. When her father was supposed to come for visits, he would not show up or he'd show up late. As a child, she forgave the first six or seven times, but then the disappointment began to build up into a long-term resentment and unforgiveness toward him.

Maybe your disappointment is not getting the job promotion you felt you deserved. Maybe the promotion went to someone who had been manipulating the boss and weasled his or her way into their favor, even though you were better qualified.

Maybe your disappointment is in your marriage. Your spouse doesn't live up to your expectations. Your marriage isn't going the way you thought it would. Maybe your life is a disappointment. You had dreams and ambitions but they have slowly fizzled and died and you feel as if your life has been wasted. Disappointment can create an attitude of unforgiveness toward those in your life. Even if they weren't the source of your disappointment, they reap the fruit of it.

Holding on to rejection

Rejection hurts deeply. It severs a tie that is meaningful to you and it hurts. A loss of love and friendship sends the message, "You aren't good enough." Rejection can be as small as a college paper being given a low grade by a teacher. It can be a job interview where you're told, "You're not qualified." Rejection can come from many different avenues: rejected for the sports team in high school, dumped by a boyfriend or girlfriend in college, divorced by your spouse.

Holding on to a feeling of abandonment

Abandonment is a real issue in our culture because of divorce, remarriage and single parenting. It is a painful and devastating experience. Children often feel abandoned when a parent leaves and starts a new family.

The fear of abandonment is a powerful force in many people's lives. It prevents them from developing relationships and taints their perspective on life. Some begin to feel that God has abandoned them. But Isaiah 49:15-16 assures us that will never happen: "Can a woman forget her nursing child, and not have compassion on the son of her womb? Surely they may forget, yet I will not forget you. See, I have inscribed you on the palms of My hands." Here, God exposes the depth of His heart toward you. He will never forget you. He will never abandon you.

Holding on to past offenses

An offense can cause a person to distrust someone whom they previously trusted. Offenses through words or actions can deeply wound a person. Being treated unjustly or with insensitivity can hurt and injure another.

The Greek word for offense is literally translated "a bait stick." This was a stick covered with a food or smell that would tempt an animal to enter a trap. It was an aroma that the animal trusted and it lured him into the trap. When it took the bait from the stick, the trap would slam shut. This "bait stick" is the image of offense. An offense happens when you are lured into trusting someone. Once you take the bait and extend your trust, the trap slams shut and you are injured. You have been baited and hurt. You have been offended.

Offenses can be major or minor. They can be small offenses that you put into your bank account and store up until the account of offense is overflowing so you draw out bitterness. Psalm 38:12 warns of people who cause offense. "Those also who seek my life lay snares for me; those who seek my hurt speak of destruction, and plan deception all day long." In a later Psalm, the writer rejoices of the power of God to overcome offenses. "Our soul has escaped as a bird from the snare of the fowlers; the snare is broken, and we have escaped" (Psalm 124:7).

People will offend you

Matthew 18:7 says, "For offenses must come." If you are alive and breathing and have any relationships with other people, offenses will come. Some are deliberate and some are accidental, but they will come.

Offenses can come from friends. Usually friends don't mean to offend, but a casual word spoken thoughtlessly can hurt, even without their realizing it. Parents can cause offenses. Children and stepchildren can cause offenses. Kids can say things out of hurt and rejection that they really don't mean. They can strike out with harsh words, "I wish you weren't my mother. You're not really my father. I hate you." As a parent, you have poured your love, life, time, energy and heart into your children and they can react to some situation with bitter words that hurt, even if you know they don't mean it.

People you work with or go to church with or go to school with can offend you. Leaders – pastors, teachers and supervisors – can cause offenses. Jesus offended the Pharisees on a regular basis. In Matthew 15:13, His disciples came to him and asked, "Knowest thou that the Pharisees were offended, after they heard this saying? But he answered and said, Every plant, which my heavenly Father hath not planted, shall be rooted up."

The beginning of an unforgiving spirit

An unforgiving spirit can begin with a feeling of being hurt, treated wrongly. The wronged person may ask, "Why did this happen to me? How could they do that? It isn't fair. I thought they were my friend. I thought they cared about me. How could they treat me that way?" They chew over the event mentally, replaying the hurt in their mind.

Next they try to avoid the pain. Maybe they drop the friendship, shut themselves off from those who hurt them. They avoid situations that remind them of the hurt. "It doesn't matter. I'll just forget it happened." But they can't forget. Deep inside it eats at them, gnawing a raw spot in their heart.

This leads to living in defeat – spiritually, mentally and emotionally. They feel as if the hurt has destroyed them and they have no hope left. They drive people away so they aren't hurt again and a sense of defeat sets in.

Living in defeat gives way to discouragement and depression. "I'll never be happy again. I'll never get over this." Depression begins in the core of the person. It creates a hardness in the spirit that changes the way a person feels, thinks and acts.

What happens? They decide not to forgive and release the past. They have an unforgiving spirit. They decide they cannot forgive; they will not forgive. They will make the other person pay. Hardness and resentment settles in and a desire for revenge drives them.

Reasons people won't forgive

You may think if you decide to forgive, your offender will never know they were wrong. You want them to know how deeply they hurt you and to see how wrong they were. You want to confront them, force them to see what they have done.

You may believe that it is unfair for the one who is hurt to have to be the one who makes it right. They caused the pain and turmoil so they need to come apologize if they want forgiveness. The problem is that scripture commands you to forgive, even if your offender has not come to you in repentance for their actions.

You may be worried that forgiving means you have to restore a relationship or friendship as it was before. If you forgive them, then you will have to reconcile with them and place yourself in the same place that caused you so much hurt before. Forgiveness does not mean that you must have a full restoration of relationship. There are times when that would be foolish and would be placing yourself in an unsafe place. You don't have to put yourself in a dangerous situation just because you forgave that person.

Lies of unforgiveness

An unforgiving person feeds off four lies. First, he blames the offender: "If this had not happened, I would have a better life." It provides an excuse for anything and everything that is wrong in the person's life. Anytime something goes wrong, the reason goes back to the source of the unforgiveness. That is the cause of every problem.

Next, the unforgiving person says, "I am a victim of an undeserved injury or injustice." He sees himself as a good person who has been taken advantage of. He judges everyone else and interprets every action they take and every word they say through that filter of victimization. He is the righteous victim who has been unfairly treated. The problem is that being a victim robs you of life. Being a victim wraps you in a cocoon of self-protection that not only protects you from hurt, but it protects you from living a full life.

The third lie the unforgiving person believes is, "I have power over you because you hurt me." No one can make him forgive. No one can force him to stop holding a grudge, so he has power over them. He can remind them of how badly they hurt him and make them keep paying until he chooses to forgive them. He can dangle his forgiveness in front of them to force them to treat him in a certain way. But if they say something he doesn't like, he will pull his forgiveness back and remind them of how wrong they were.

Unforgiveness is like a wall of thorns that you plant around your life. . . .The thorns get longer and sharper until the day comes that you realize the thorns you planted to protect you from hurt have now imprisoned you.

The unforgiving person also says, "I will never be hurt again." Not forgiving protects you from being hurt again, both by the person who hurt you originally and also by any new people in your life. It keeps the pain alive, making you overly sensitive to each potential danger. It is a shield that pushes people away and keeps them at arm's length. It reduces the risk of ever again being rejected, deceived or abused.

Unforgiveness is like a wall of thorns that you plant around your life. It protects you from those who would harm you. Any time someone gets close enough to touch you, you pull back behind that wall and you are protected and secure from further injury.

But the wall of thorns grows with time. It grows higher and thicker. The thorns get longer and sharper until the day comes that you realize the thorns that you planted around you to protect you from hurt have now imprisoned you. You are no longer able to get out, no longer able to touch others, no longer able to receive love. You are trapped in the thorny prison of unforgiveness, not just isolated from pain but isolated from love.

Degrees of unforgiveness

Maybe you are willing to forgive but only to a certain extent. You can forgive someone but make a mental decision to mark their offense. You remember the wrong that has been done to you and brand it into your memory. Anytime they do something else hurtful, that old memory pops up and says, "Remember, this isn't the first time they've hurt you. Don't forget when they did ..." It's a mental unforgiveness that keeps track of every wrong committed.

Emotional unforgiveness is when the mental record you are keeping works its way out of your mind and into your heart. It begins to affect your emotions, and resentment sets in. You begin to find fault with the person and be critical of them.

Finally, it can settle into full unforgiveness. Your unforgiveness moves past your mind and emotions and settles into your spirit. The core part of your life is now infected with bitterness. It affects your personality and every aspect of your life. Even when you aren't thinking about the incident, the bitterness touches every area of your life because it has become part of who you are.

Chapter 5

The Self-Defeat of Withholding Forgiveness

J oe was dying. Years earlier he had a falling out with his former best friend, Bill. It had been a foolish disagreement, but it had festered for years, fed by many sharp and harsh words. Now Joe was dying and he didn't want to die with this broken relationship, so he sent for Bill.

When Bill arrived, Joe told him he didn't want to die harboring bad feelings for him and, reluctantly and with great effort, Joe apologized for the things he had said and done. In return, he also forgave Bill for his offenses as well. As Bill finally turned to leave the room, Joe called out to him, "One more thing, Bill. Remember, if I get better, this doesn't count!"

How often have we said words of forgiveness without changing the spirit of unforgiveness? Maybe we aren't as blunt about it as Joe was, but we still do it.

The hidden attitudes of unforgiveness

Unworthiness

This is shame-based self-hatred. It is a sense of self-rejection, an inner voice that tells you that you are no good and something is wrong with you. You compare yourself to others and believe you have more problems than most people.

Perfectionism

You always try to prove your worth and to gain love and acceptance through performance. You need to always do things a little bit better. You strive to make no mistakes, not from a desire for excellence but from a fear of being wrong. You believe that if you examine yourself closely, you will find many terrible things inside. You try to be perfect on the outside to hide the problems on the inside.

Supersensitivity

You are very touchy, easily offended by people's words. Even the most casual statement can be misinterpreted and deepen the offense. An example of supersensitivity would be that of the two former friends who ran into each other at a New Year's party. Because of some offense that had happened, neither one had said a good word to each other or about each other for the past year. A mutual friend tried to convince them that the end of the year was a good time to put old offenses behind them and begin the new year with forgiveness. But neither one would have anything to do with it.

Finally, the friend asked in frustration, "Couldn't you at least wish him one thing for the next year? Just one?" Reluctantly, one man said, "Okay, for the next year I wish him whatever he would wish for me." Immediately the other man shouted angrily, "You see? He can't say anything nice to me!"

Negative attitude

A person who harbors unforgiveness lives in negativity. He assumes the worst and lives with a victim mentality that expects people to mistreat them. God has great plans on the horizon of his life, but he will never see them if he lives with unforgiveness in his heart. God cannot use a person who cannot forgive.

Bitterness

The seed of unforgiveness grows into a root of bitterness that taints every part of a person's life. Bitterness comes from holding onto the minor offenses and harboring the hurt within. Hebrews

12:15-16 warns us to "look carefully lest anyone fall short of the grace of God; lest any root of bitterness springing up cause trouble, and by this many become defiled."

Enslavement

Being unable to forgive someone causes you to be controlled by the person who hurt you. This is especially true if you hold the mistaken belief that you cannot forgive until the offender asks for your forgiveness and apologizes or makes restitution. That is like locking yourself in a cell and handing your tormenter the key. Your emotions and actions have become totally dependent on what the person who hurt you chooses to do. They now control you.

Two ex-inmates from a Nazi concentration camp were talking about their experiences. One asked, "Have you forgiven the Nazis?" His friend erupted in anger, "No, I haven't! I am still consumed with hatred for them!" The first man replied, "In that case, they still have you in prison."

Shaming the offender

You can offer forgiveness to someone but with a clause that states your superiority over them. "I forgive you. After all I should have known you are too immature to understand what you did." Or you can offer forgiveness in a manner that heaps guilt upon them. "My life has been destroyed by what you did and I will never recover. I will forgive you but don't forget what you have done to me."

The unforgiving spirit at work

The unforgiving spirit holds a person hostage. It makes love and acceptance contingent upon the other person's actions. It withholds respect and service until it is satisfied. The only problem is that unforgiveness is never satisfied.

The unforgiving spirit cannot be limited to one relationship or situation. The bitterness and resentment will spill over into other relationships and destroy them as well. A person who has been offended and will not forgive becomes overly sensitive to every slight that may be given to them. The anger may have originated toward a spouse, but it will explode upon the children. The bitterness may be directed towards a boss, but it will spill over onto the co-workers. The attitude of unforgiveness will touch every area of life and tarnish all relationships, not just the original offending party.

Signs of unresolved offenses

Strained Relationships

Proverbs 18:19 says, "A brother offended is harder to win than a strong city, and contentions are like the bars of a castle." If you are offended at someone, your relationship with them is harmed. You hold them at arm's length. Everything they say or do passes through the filter of that offense and aggravates the problem.

Resisting Authority

Offenses cause distrust and hinder your response to authority. An offended person does not trust people because they have been hurt by them. That distrust filters and interprets authority in view of those hurts. Hebrews 13:17 says, "Obey those who rule over you, and be submissive, for they watch out for your souls, as those who must give account. Let them do so with joy and not with grief, for that would be unprofitable to you."

God has set leaders in place as safeguards and protection. They are not there to harm, but for your benefit.

A person who has been offended will often pull back from strained relationships and begin to withdraw. Eventually they begin to drift away from the place where God has planted them, their local church. They quit going to church because they don't want to have to face the person who has caused them pain. Eventually they leave and drift from place to place, looking for a church where they will not be offended and hurt. Unfortunately, there is no such place.

In Scripture, Christians are likened to trees. Psalm 92:12-13 says, "The righteous shall flourish like a palm tree, he shall grow like a cedar in Lebanon. Those who are planted in the house of the Lord shall flourish in the courts of our God." (See also Psalm 1:3, 52:8.)

Trees have an interesting reaction to wind. When a tree grows in a windy area, stress is created on the tree. In response, the tree changes its growth pattern and begins to lay down cells in a spiral pattern. This results in a tree that is stronger and more flexible. If a tree is wounded, it heals fastest along the areas where it has been stressed by the wind.

In the same way, a person who has experienced the stress of being offended and then forgiving is one who becomes stronger. The grain of their life begins to wind around the grace of God and they become more flexible and can handle stress easier than one who has never responded to the dealings of

God through others. They have also learned a grace that enables them to heal more quickly.

Strongholds of vain imaginations

The trauma of an offense may cause people to become emotionally unstable and they begin to see every situation and circumstance through the frame of their offense. One real offense can give rise to many perceived offenses.

2 Corinthians 10:3-4 tells us, "For though we walk in the flesh, we do not war according to the flesh. For the weapons of our warfare are not carnal but mighty in God for pulling down strongholds." Remember, your struggle is not against a person but against unforgiveness in your heart. 2 Corinthians promises us that through God you can pull down that stronghold and begin to forgive.

Constant satanic harassment

Ephesians 4:26-27 warns us, "Be angry, and do not sin: do not let the sun go down on your wrath, nor give place to the devil." Don't leave a foothold for the devil. Don't provide an opportunity for him to plant a seed of resentment into your spirit. Unresolved offenses open the door for him to enter other areas of your life, spreading the anger until it affects your whole person.

The river of the Holy Spirit within you dries up

If you are offended at a person, you plug up the well of the Spirit within you. Refusing to forgive will destroy you more quickly than you can destroy the person who has wronged you. Remember, Mark 11:26 tells us, "If you do not forgive, neither will your Father in heaven forgive your trespasses." The Spirit cannot flow through an unforgiving heart.

If you have a spirit of unforgiveness, your eyes become fixed on yourself and your problems. You see everything in light of your own hurt. You lose your sensitivity to others because you feel only your own pain. You no longer look to serve others because you are the victim, the wounded person, and others should serve you. And the gifts of God lie dormant within you, unable to be expressed through the barrier of unforgiveness.

A critical attitude

A person who is unforgiving develops a critical and divisive attitude. They find fault with everyone and everything. They don't see it as being critical, but as the ability to "see things the way they are."

They stand on the high ground and look down at others around them and find all their faults and flaws, big and small.

Do you have a critical attitude? Ask yourself these questions.

1) Are you an expert in finding fault with others?
2) Do you keep a mental list of people's faults and remind them whenever you have the opportunity?
3) Do you think it is normal to be cynical?
4) Do you use sarcasm in most of your conversations?
5) Are you pessimistic about other people's projects?
6) When someone wants to know why something might not work, do they call you?
7) Are you better at criticizing than finding solutions?
8) Do you think criticism is a solution?
9) Do you move up the ladder of success by pulling others off?
10) Do you like showing contempt for other people's ideas?
11) Is mocking a fun pass-time?

12) Do you patronize people who work for or with you?
13) Do you have trouble in brainstorming sessions because you feel the need to analyze each idea?
14) Do you believe prayer is an opportunity to complain to God?

Hope for the unforgiving

If you find yourself in any of these areas of unforgiveness, you can still develop a heart of mercy. It may seem difficult. It may seem overwhelming, but the same God that pours out His grace upon us and gives us forgiveness is the God who extends to us the grace to forgive others. When you reach out to forgive, you do not reach out alone for the God of forgiveness is with you.

The poet Edwin Markham learned that the man who had been entrusted with his retirement portfolio had squandered his money. His life's savings were gone and he had nothing to fall back on. First anger, then unforgiveness settled in. He fretted about the future and resentfully fumed about his friend's offense until he concluded one day, "I must forgive him. I *will* forgive him."

Markham penned these words: "He drew a circle to shut me out, heretic, rebel, a thing to flout. But love and I had the wit to win, we drew a circle to take him in."[8] He extended grace to encompass the offense and found forgiveness.

Chapter 6

The Heart of a Forgiving Person

We can live snared or we can live as described in Psalm 124:7, "Our soul has escaped as a bird from the snare of the fowlers; the snare is broken and we have escaped." You can escape the trap of unforgiveness.

Developing an attitude of forgiveness

Are you ready to forgive? Do you approach life with an attitude that is naturally inclined toward forgiveness? We don't have to convince God to forgive us. We don't have to twist His arm. Psalm 86:5 says God is eager to forgive: "For You, Lord, are good, and ready to forgive, and abundant in mercy to all those who call upon You."

We don't have to offer all sorts of promises and guarantees to get His forgiveness. He is ready to forgive. Is that your attitude? Do you make people pay to get your forgiveness or do you freely give it?

A person with a forgiving spirit is willing to let go of hurts that have been nurtured for a long time, willing to confess and own up to the fault that is his. A heart that is ready to forgive is one that is ready to issue a pardon before the offense happens. A forgiving spirit has a predisposition to forgive. It is the first response and an automatic decision.

A person who resolves offenses has strong relationships. People who forgive develop deep friendships because they are willing to overlook offenses. They don't waste time with gossip, murmuring, criticism or tearing down others. Instead they are people of encouragement whom others love to be around.

A person who resolves offenses serves others. They have the capacity to focus their energy on serving others and reaching out to them because they are not weighed down with offenses and hurts. They have the ability to heal the broken and lift up the downcast.

Releasing the burden

There is a story of two monks who were walking into town from their monastery. As they approached a stream, an elderly woman stopped them. "Sirs, the water is swift and the stones are slippery. I'm old and tend to stumble and I'm afraid to cross alone in case I slip and am swept downstream by the current.

Could you help me?" The older monk smiled gently, "Of course, we will. Sit in the cradle we make of our hands and we will carry you so your feet do not get wet." Thankfully the woman allowed them to carry her across the stream and deposit her safely on the other side.

They strode off at a quick pace, leaving the woman far behind and then the young monk spoke. "I never thought an old woman could be so heavy. My back is still hurting from carrying her. It doesn't help that my robe is now soaked because I couldn't lift it as we crossed the stream, so now it is weighing me down too." He continued grumbling as they walked. Finally he looked at the older monk and complained, "What about you? Didn't carrying her wear you out?" The older monk shook his head, "No, because I stopped carrying her after we crossed the stream."

A person with the spirit of forgiveness lays down the burden and moves on. A person with the spirit of resentment and offense carries the burden far longer than he should and has no energy or desire left to serve others. The spirit of forgiveness blesses others while the spirit of offenses blames and criticizes them.

Activating a forgiving spirit

A person with a forgiving spirit has accepted the forgiveness of God for their sin and has forgiven themselves by trusting in God's grace. 1 John 1:9 promises, "If we confess our sins, He is faithful and just to forgive us our sins and to cleanse us from all unrighteousness."

Paul gives us a picture of forgiveness in Colossians 2:13-14: "And you, being dead in your trespasses and the uncircumcision of your flesh, He has made alive together with Him, having forgiven you all trespasses, having wiped out the handwriting of requirements that was against us, which was contrary to us. And He has taken it out of the way, having nailed it to the cross."

A forgiving spirit by faith sets others free from any obligation they have because they wronged or hurt you. When you forgive someone, you release them from any debt that you may think they owe you because of the offense. Forgiveness is a gift with no strings attached.

You don't hold that offense over their head and require that they be punished before you forgive them. Forgiveness sees the hand of God at work through imperfect people and surrenders to God, accepting His grace for the pain that life can bring.

A forgiving spirit seeks God for a turning point in the cycle of unforgiveness, resentment and bitterness. Forgiveness is not easy, but if you do not forgive, resentment quickly follows. You cannot afford to nurture resentment and bitterness. Forgiveness turns to God for the strength and the grace that is needed to forgive.

> When you forgive someone, you release them from any debt that you may think they owe you because of the offense. Forgiveness is a gift with no strings attached.

In his book *Like Christ*, Andrew Murray said,

"To forgive like you, blessed Son of God! I take this as the law of my life. You who have given me the command, give also the power. You who have

loved enough to forgive me, will also fill me with love and teach me to forgive others. You who gave me the first blessings, in the joy of having my sins forgiven, will surely give me the second blessing, a deeper joy, of forgiving others as you have forgiven me. Fill me with the faith in the power of your love in me to make me like yourself, to enable me to forgive the seventy times seven."[9]

A forgiving spirit takes responsibility to turn the situation around for the offenses and the damage done. We need to cleanse our offense with God, but it doesn't stop there. We must accept full responsibility for the person we have hurt, offended or taken advantage of. We must go and ask forgiveness, make it right and clear our conscience (Acts 24:16).

In Matthew 5:22-24 the responsibility for resolving offenses is placed on the one who has hurt or offended someone. "If you bring your gift to the altar, and remember that your brother has something against you, leave your gift there before the altar, and go your way. First be reconciled to your brother, and then come and offer your gift." If you know you have offended someone, it is your responsibility to go to them and to be reconciled. It may not be easy but God's grace will be with you.

A person with a forgiving spirit takes the responsibility to resolve offenses even when others have caused the offense. If you have been offended, don't start pointing fingers at the person who offended you and demanding that they come grovel at your feet and beg forgiveness. Matthew 18:15 places the burden of reconciliation on you. "If a fellow believer hurts you, go and tell him – work it out between the two of you. If he listens, you've made a friend." (*The Message Bible*) It is your responsibility to work on reconciliation. So whether you have been offended or if you have caused offense, the responsibility is yours to resolve it.

A person with a forgiving spirit takes the responsibility to resolve offenses even when others have caused the offense.

Having a forgiving spirit allows God to reveal to you those individuals who have allowed unforgiveness and bitterness because of your offense. As you come before God, allow Him to reveal to you those who have been hurt because of you. Determine to clean up all past offenses as soon as possible. Don't blame-shift or make excuses.

Don't use terminology that would have you assume anything less than full responsibility for what you have done wrong: "I've offended you, but..." "I'm wrong but you were, too." "If I'm wrong..." "If I hurt you..." Be up front and acknowledge what you did.

A forgiving spirit uses wisdom in resolving offenses. Sometimes offenses can be resolved without going to the other person. Colossians 3:13 challenges us to "bear with one another and forgive one another, if anyone has a complaint against another; even as Christ forgave you, so you also must do." Sometimes a person offends out of immaturity or ignorance. They never intended to do wrong. They have no idea that they said anything that was hurtful so we must choose to "bear with them," forgiving them without confronting.

These can be isolated instances that are not likely to be repeated. They only affect you and no one else. Maybe it was one comment in the middle of a sermon or one side-comment during a conversation. So you forgive quietly and let it go.

Sometimes an offense can be overlooked because it is a personality conflict. Maybe your mother laughs too loud at the wrong time. Perhaps your father tells too many stories and bores you to tears. Maybe your sister dresses differently than you think is appropriate. Your friend has a sense of humor that is different than yours. Don't allow offense to settle in, but overlook the personality differences and allow them to be who they are, just as they allow you to be who you are.

Mother Teresa had a poem hanging on her wall that makes this point very clearly.

People are often unreasonable,
illogical and self-centered;
Forgive them anyway.

If you are kind,
People may accuse you
of selfish, ulterior motives;
Be kind anyway.

If you are successful,
you will win some false friends and
some true enemies;
Succeed anyway.

People may cheat you;
Be honest and frank anyway.

What you spend years building,
someone could destroy overnight;
Build anyway

If you find serenity and happiness,
they may be jealous;
Be happy anyway.

The good you do today,
people will often forget tomorrow;
Do good anyway.

Give the world the best you have,
and it may never be enough;
Give the world the best you've got anyway.

You see, in the final analysis.
it is between you and God;
It is never between you and them anyway.

Removing the weight of unforgiveness

A teacher wanted to give her students an unforgettable picture of the reality of not forgiving. When they came to class, each of them brought a plastic bag and a sack of potatoes. They were instructed to write the name and date of every person in life who had offended them that they had not forgiven and put those potatoes in their bag.

For the next month they carried that bag with them everywhere. As they put that bag beside their bed at night, tossed it into the passenger seat of their car, dragged it into the office and kicked it under their desk, those with a full load of potatoes were beginning to regret their decision to not forgive.

Of course, the potatoes eventually began to rot and the students discovered that everywhere they went they were accompanied by a foul smell. At the end of the month, the students were asked what they learned. The answer was unanimous—not forgiving didn't bother the person whose name was written on that potato but the person carrying that potato sack of unforgiveness paid for it daily.

Don't carry your rotten potatoes of unforgiveness around your whole life. Don't let a cloud of bitterness follow you, tainting the atmosphere in which you live. Refusing to forgive costs you more than it costs the person who offended you. Forgiving releases you and brings freedom to your life.

Dave Pelzer wrote the book *A Child Called It*, in which he told of the horrific life he led as a child. While his mother cared for his siblings, she heaped abuse upon Dave, starving him, beating him, burning him. Instead of calling him by name, she only referred to him as "It" as she physically tortured and mentally abused him. Yet as an adult he said, ""We harbor ill feelings in our heart, and over time, [if we don't forgive] we become a carbon copy of what we once hated."[10]

Prayer of forgiveness

Think of those people who have hurt you. It may be in large ways or in small ways, but they have offended you and caused you harm. Make a decision to forgive them. Remember, forgiveness is a decision, not an emotion. Make a deliberate choice to forgive and pray this prayer:

"Dear Heavenly Father, I thank You for the riches of Your kindness that have led me to repentance. I confess that I have not shown that same kindness toward those who have hurt me. Instead, I have held on to bitterness

and resentment. Please bring to my mind all the people I need to forgive in order that I may now do so."

"Lord, I choose to forgive_____(name the person) for_____(what he/she did or failed to do), which made me feel _____(share the painful feelings)."

"Lord, I choose not to hold on to my resentment. I thank You for setting me free from the bondage of my bitterness. I relinquish my right to seek revenge and ask You to heal my damaged emotions. I now ask You to bless those who have hurt me. In Jesus' name, amen." [11]

Forgiveness: Releasing the Power of Grace

Chapter 7

Responding With Love to Life Experiences

Life isn't fair. Even kindergarteners quickly learn that lesson. Sometimes things happen in life that simply aren't right and aren't fair. These are the contradictions in life, the times when bad things happen to good people and good things happen to bad people.

What do you do when your family hurts you, your best friend disappoints you, your spouse walks out on you, your employer discriminates against you, your coworkers lie about you? What do you do?

Did you do as Joseph did when the brothers who had sold him out came begging for mercy? "But as for you, you meant evil against me; but God meant it for good, in order to bring it about as it is this day, to save many people."

Joseph saw that there is a God. There is a purpose. There is a sovereignty and destiny that eclipses the difficulties in life. He saw the cruelty, the injustice, the rejection, the pits and prison, the lies and abuse through the sovereignty of God and found purpose and destiny in them. He didn't look only at what man did, but at what God did with that.

God has used all that has happened to you, both good and bad, to make you a unique person. He has used your experiences to form you into a vessel that He can use to bless others.

God has used all that has happened to you, both good and bad, to make you a unique person. He has used your experiences to form you into a vessel that He can use to bless others. The heart of a forgiving person believes that God is sovereign in His dealings and that He makes every circumstance work for good—even those that look bad and undeserved at the time. A forgiving person knows that God sent us where we are. God manages all the events of our lives, including the difficult ones. God allows us to go through painful seasons to learn from them.

The forgiving person does not focus on the person who caused the hurt but on the God who brings good from it. Your life does not belong to you, but to a living God who is in control of every situation. That person who harmed you may have been part of your life, but they do not control it. God does. They may have meant to harm you, but God intends to bless you through it.

Make Romans 8:28 a part of your life philosophy and not just words on paper. "And we know. . ." We know. We don't guess. We don't hope. We know. We are convinced and no situation that comes against us can shatter that confidence. We stake our life on it.

"We know that all things work together for good." The Greek word used here is sunergeo, which means working together or to engage in an activity together with someone else. It can be translated, "God coworking provides all things for good or so that it is well with them."[13]

Your circumstances aren't working by themselves, wreaking havoc on your life. God is working with them and using them. He is engaged in activity with your situations to bring good into your life.

"We are assured and know that [God being a partner in their labor] all things work together and are fitting into a plan for good to and for those who love God and are called according to His design and purpose" (Romans 8:28, *The Amplified Bible*).

Breaking points become grace encounters

Breaking points will come in your life. They may be points of rejection, disappointment, cruelty, hurt, or despair. There will be things that life will throw your way with the potential to break you and to crush your spirit. Sometimes they are unexpected breaking points: the doctor says, "Terminal cancer." The policeman says, "Your child is hurt." Your boss says, "You're fired." They are unexpected words that hit you with the force of a hurricane and drive your breath from you. You are driven to your knees in despair.

Breaking points can be progressive. The pressure builds over time and your strength is slowly drained until you slowly begin to sink to the ground, unable to stand. You've prayed for years for your son but he is in prison again and you don't know what to do. You've intervened for your daughter and checked her into rehab time and time again but this time she has OD'd and is in a coma in the hospital. You've hit your limit. You are broken. Your strength is gone.

Greatness comes from the breaking points in life. The greatness of Joseph was the brokenness of his spirit. His humility came from the pit, the prison, the rejection, the loneliness. The greatness of the man did not come when Pharaoh made him prime minister. The greatness came out of what happened in his spirit during those breaking point seasons. His greatness grew every time he made a decision to forgive, every time he made a decision to remain pliable in the hand of God, every time he grabbed hold of God's grace instead of giving way to bitterness.

Joseph learned in the worst moments of life how to hold on to the grace of God. He learned grace in the breaking points of life. Malcolm Muggeridge also discovered that affliction brought understanding:

> *"Contrary to what might be expected, I look back on experiences that at the time seemed especially desolating and painful with particular satisfaction. Indeed, I can say with complete truthfulness that everything I have learned in my 75 years in this world, everything that has truly enhanced and enlightened my experience, has been through affliction and not through happiness."*[14]

A softened heart from hard experiences

When you go through hard experiences, they will either make you harder or they will make you softer. The same rain that softens the ground can harden it. The same fire that warms a house can also destroy it. It is your choice. The way that you respond to the events of life and the situations that you go through will determine your heart condition.

When Joseph saw his brothers for the first time in thirteen years, he wept. Genesis 43:30 says, "Now his heart yearned for his brother, so Joseph made haste and sought somewhere to weep. And he went into his chamber and wept there." There was a softness, a humility, a brokenness in his spirit.

When the time came that he told his brothers who he was, he could have lambasted them. He could have told them how they had hurt him, how he had suffered, described his years of imprisonment, the beatings, the hunger, the loneliness. Instead Genesis 45:15 says that "he kissed all his brothers and wept over them, and after that his brothers talked with him." He still loved his brothers after all they had done. Only a soft heart can love those who have caused harm.

The amazing thing is that Joseph went one step further. He invited — more than invited, he urged them — to move in next door so that he could take care of them. They had rejected him; he wanted them near to protect them.

Responding to hate with love

A similar situation happened in Laos, where a handful of Christians lived in a Laotian village. The men worked in the fields together. The women washed their clothes together. Their children played together. One day the quiet village was filled with sounds of shouting as these once-friendly neighbors threw rocks at the Christians and demanded "Kill them! Kill them!" Phong had pastored that church from its inception. He had lived among these people and knew they were crying out for his and his family's deaths.

God intervened that day and they were not killed, but they were thrown into prison until they gave up their faith. As they were marched to the trucks waiting to take them to jail, their friends, their neighbors, their relatives jabbed them in the back with sticks, threw stones, spit on them and chanted over and over "Kill them!"

When Phong was released from jail, he had a choice. What did he do now? He went back to his village and walked into his neighbor's house, "I forgive you. What has happened is past and is not important. We are neighbors. We are friends. Let us forget what has happened and continue to live at peace as friends and neighbors." He had a choice – forgive or hate, become hard or soft. He became soft and more of his village became Christians.

Refusing to live in the pain of the past

While Joseph was in Egypt, he had two children and he named them prophetically. He called the first one Manasseh, which means "causing to forget" because "God has made me to forget all my toil and all my father's house" (Genesis 41:51). Joseph chose not to live in the pain of yesterday, and neither should you. You do not have to live with the shadows of the past haunting you daily. Leave them in the past and forget them.

To forget them does not mean that you are unable to remember. It means that you let go of the memory and do not hold to it. Our English word "forget" comes from a Germanic word meaning "to lose one's grasp on." You don't hold those memories tightly in your fist, but you open your hand and allow the wind of the Spirit to blow through them. They are not erased, but they are loosened. Even though you remember, you are not overwhelmed with a knot in your stomach and ache in your heart. The memory is there but it no longer controls you and how you view life.

You can hold onto your resentment and unforgiveness or you can allow God to remove the pain so that you can begin to walk in fruitfulness.

A lady once showed an artist an expensive handkerchief on which a blot of ink had been dropped. "It's ruined," she complained and threw it away. The artist said nothing but quietly removed the handkerchief from the trash can. A little while later the lady received her handkerchief back, but so changed she could hardly believe it was the original. Using the ink blot as the basis, the artist had worked around it a beautiful and artistic design, changing what was ruined into a thing of beauty and joy.

In the same way God can work with the ink blot in your life, transforming it with His grace. The ink blot is still there. The hurt from the past has not ceased to exist, but it can be so transformed through the grace of God that it has gained an eternal beauty. The hurts, disappointments and failures that appear to you as overwhelming and threaten to destroy your life can become a thing of grace in the hands of God.

Forgiveness opens the way to fruitfulness

Joseph named his second son Ephraim, which means "double fruitfulness" because "God has caused me to be fruitful in the land of my affliction" (Genesis 41:52). He had to have Manasseh (forgetting) before he could have Ephraim. God cannot bless you and bring fruitfulness if you are wallowing in bitterness.

The Laotian pastor mentioned earlier has seen his church grow since his imprisonment. That would not have happened if he had held onto his resentment for the way he had been treated. When he responded with grace and love toward his neighbors, he opened the door for God to bring blessing into his life.

You have the choice now. You can hold onto your resentment and unforgiveness or you can allow God to remove the pain so that you can begin to walk in fruitfulness. He has a great destiny for you, a future that is full of the goodness of God. You choose.

At his death, Joseph's father gave Joseph an extra portion of interitance as a reward for his graciousness toward his brothers. In the same way, God will reward you with supernatural surprises. He will give you extra grace, extra provision, extra blessings. I believe a forgiving person has a more abundant life because of the grace on his or her life through responding correctly to the dealings of God.

The choice is yours

Imagine this scene from a courtroom trial in South Africa: A frail black woman rises slowly to her feet. She is over 70 years of age. Facing her from across the room are several white security police officers, one of whom, Mr. van der Broek, has just been tried and found guilty in the murders of both the woman's son and her husband some years before.

It was indeed Mr. van der Broek, it has now been established, who had come to the woman's home a number of years back, taken her son, shot him at point-blank range and then burned the young man's body while he and his officers partied nearby.

Several years later, van der Broek and his cohorts had returned to take away her husband as well. For many months she heard nothing of his where-abouts. Then, almost two years after her husband's disappearance, van der Broek came back to fetch the woman herself. How vividly she remembers that evening, going to a place beside a river where she was shown her husband, bound and beaten, but still strong in spirit, lying on a pile of wood. The last words she heard from his lips as the officers poured gasoline over his body and set him aflame were, "Father, forgive them."

And now the woman stands in the courtroom and listens to the confessions offered by Mr. van der Broek. A member of South Africa's Truth and Reconciliation Commission turns to her and asks, "So, what do you want? How should justice be done to this man who has so brutally destroyed your family?"

"I want three things," begins the old woman, calmly but confidently. "I want first to be taken to the place where my husband's body was burned so that I can gather up the dust and give his remains a decent burial." She pauses, then continues. "My husband and son were my only family.

"I want, secondly, therefore, for Mr. van der Broek to become my son. I would like for him to come twice a month to the ghetto and spend a day with me so that I can pour out on him whatever love I still have remaining within me.

"And, finally," she says, "I want a third thing. I would like Mr. van der Broek to know that I offer him my forgiveness because Jesus Christ died to forgive. This was also the wish of my husband. And so, I would kindly ask someone to come to my side and lead me across the courtroom so that I can take Mr. van der Broek in my arms, embrace him and let him know that he is truly forgiven."

As the court assistants come to lead the elderly woman across the room, Mr. van der Broek, overwhelmed by what he has just heard, faints. And as he does, those in the courtroom, friends, family, neighbors — all victims of decades of oppression and injustice — begin to sing, softly, but assuredly, "Amazing grace, how sweet the sound, that saved a wretch like me."[12]

Forgiveness is a choice, a choice that this woman made. It is a choice that you must make too. It isn't just a crisis choice, to be made only when an overwhelming situation befalls you. It is a daily choice that is made over and over through the small offenses that come your way.

Your first choice is the choice to accept God's forgiveness for you. No matter what you have done, His blood covers your sin. He holds His hand out to you offering forgiveness; all you have to do is take His hand. It's your choice.

Your second choice is the choice to extend that same forgiveness to others. It isn't always easy but it is always necessary. It's a deliberate choice. Your emotions may not quickly follow your decision, but they will. Corrie Ten Boom compares forgiveness with ringing a church bell. Unforgiveness keeps pulling on the rope and causing the bell to ring. When you forgive, you release the rope, but the bell will still continue to toll a few more times before it is silent.

Make a decision to let go of the rope. The emotions may still flare up for awhile, but silence and peace will come. Make the decision to no longer hold that person in judgment. Decide to see the hand of

God working in every circumstance and situation and to trust Him.

It's your decision. Choose a forgiving heart.

Forgiveness: Releasing the Power of Grace

EndNotes

1 Anne Graham Lotz, Just Give Me Jesus (Nashville, TN: Word Publishing, 2000), pp. 279-280.

2 John Reaves, Sr. "The Strange Case of George Wilson," The Baptist Pillar (Bible Baptist Church, 1203 4th St. Brandon, MB Canada). http://www.baptistpillar.com/bd0509.htm. 13 February 2007.

3 Oswald Chambers. My Utmost for His Highest. (Grand Rapids, MI: Discovery House Publishers), December 8.

4 Andrew Murray. Like Christ. (http://www.jesus.org.uk/vault/library/murray_like_christ.pdf), 14 February 2007.

5 Dr. Barry Lubetkin. (www.sober.org/ForgVict.html), 11 December 2003.

6 Charlotte vanOyen Witvliet. "Practicing Forgiveness: What Happens Emotionally and Physically When We Forgive," Preaching Forgiveness Conference. (Calvin Theological Seminary, April 27, 2005). http://www.calvin.edu/worship/resources/forgive/forgive3.php.

7 Ed Ritchie. "Forgiveness Can Be Healthy," National Fibromyalgia Association. (http://www.fmaware.org/patient/coping/forgiveness.htm). 14 February 2007.

8 Edwin Markham. "Brainy Quotes." (http://www.brainyquote.com/quotes/quotes/ e/edwinmarkh121804.html).

9 Andrew Murray. Like Christ. (http://www.jesus.org.uk/vault/library/ murray_like_christ.pdf), 14 February 2007.

10 Dave Pelzer. "How to Get Rid of the Garbage in Your Life" (http://www.oprah.com/tows/pastshows/tows_2002/tows_past_20020130_e.jhtml)

11 Neil T. Anderson. The Steps to Freedom in Christ. (Gospel Light Publishing, 2001), p. 19-22.

12 James Krabill. "Keep the Faith, Share the Peace," the newsletter of the Mennonite Church Peace and Justice Committee, Volume 5 number 3, June, 1999.

13 Thayer's Greek Lexicon. (Electronic Database, copyright (c) 2000 by Biblesoft).

14 "Suffering," (http://www.sermonillustrations.com/a-z/s/suffering.htm), 2 March 2007.

Imagine

Believe in the Power of a Dream

In this book, author Frank Damazio challenges you to rise above the limitations you place on yourself and to pursue the dream God has put in your heart. Begin with a foundation of faith—"the substance of things hoped for"—and then lift up your eyes to imagine and grasp God's desire for your future. Learn the steps to living life with vision and perseverance.

Hardcover, 4¾" x 6½", 128 pages
ISBN 13: 978-1-59383-037-3

FAX 503.257.2228 • EMAIL order@CityChristianPublishing.com

BAGGAGE

*Leaving Your
Past Behind*

Many of us get weighed down with baggage full of old memories, regrets, and hurts that we drag with us through the years. This baggage keeps us from reaching our goals, obstructs our relationships, and trips us up when we try to move forward. In this book, you'll learn to identify what's in your bag, then discover how to let it go and experience the freedom of God's grace.

*Hardcover, 4¾" x 6½", 128 pages
ISBN 13: 978-1-59383-038-0*

FAX 503.257.2228 • EMAIL order@CityChristianPublishing.com

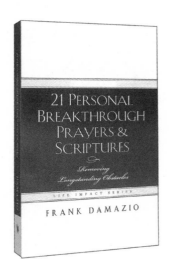

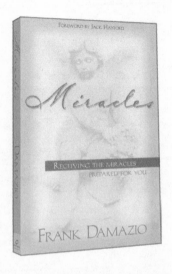

MIRACLES

*Receiving the Miracles
Prepared for You*

God desires to bring miracles into your life, and you can prepare for them with an open heart through the guidelines presented in this book. This book will inspire your faith, renew your hope, and capture your heart. Frank Damazio not only lays out a clear biblical teaching of miracles, but also provides true-life examples of miracles recorded in his miracle journal.

Softcover, 6" X 9", 272 pages
1-886849-83-8

PHONE 1.800.777.6057 • WEB www.CityChristianPublishing.com

THE HEART ALL LEADERS MUST DEVELOP

Cultivating the Nature of Christ

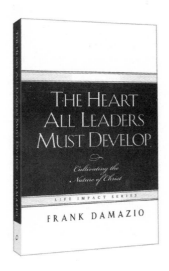

God is seeking leaders for His kingdom who minister from Christ-like hearts. This book presents the heart qualifications of leadership that all Christians must have: The heart of a father, the heart of a servant, and the heart of a shepherd. If you are a Christian leader, these are your prerequisites and the foundation of your ministry.

Hardcover, 4¾" x 6½", 138 pages
1-59383-031-9

FAX 503.257.2228 • EMAIL order@CityChristianPublishing.com